hen it was originally published in August 1985, Viz Comic No. 13 became the 13th issue of Viz Comic to be published. In the year that followed another 5 issues appeared, numbers 14, 15, 16, 17 and 18, bringing the total for that year to 6, and the overall total published to 18 (three times the total for that one year). So, in a year that had contained 12 months, half-a-dozen comics were produced.

Unlike the previous 12 issues of Viz Comic, numbers 13 to 18, if added together, would make 93. Indeed, if you add 6 to that total (because that's the number of issues included) you get 99 — just one short of a hundred, and also a popular kind of ice cream.

And now those 6 issues, all long since sold out, are brought together by popular demand in one big hardback edition, priced £5.95. Ironic indeed when you consider that 5.95 added to 15.5 (the average of 13, 14, 15, 16, 17 and 18) and then multiplied by 6 (the number of issues featured) comes to 128.7, which, rounded down, comes to 128 — the exact number of pages in this book.

LeTTeRBoX

Onion Eating

While cooking a meal for my husband recently I stopped to eat a pickled onion. I have had several more since and enjoyed them all.

Next week I intend to buy a new jar.

Mrs S. Hunter
Macclesfield

Tell us about your crazy food fettishes. A fiver for the best letter.

YOU ASK WE ANSWER

I have often wondered why trains go faster than buses.

Mrs. E. Edwards
Cheltenham

Well Mrs Edwards, that certainly is a puzzler. We rang British Rail enquiries who told us that modern trains can travel at anything up to 125 mph (Miles per hour).

Buses however are subject to the national speed restriction of 70 mph (60 mph on a single carriageway) and 30 mph in a built up area, i.e. one in which the street lights are less than 200 feet apart.

You can send your questions to 'You Ask, We Answer', PO Box 1PT, Newcastle upon Tyne, NE1 1PT. But the chances are we won't answer them.

Several years ago when I broke a mirror I remembered the superstition about '7 years bad luck'.

Two years later I entered a competition to win a holiday for two in Paris. Needless to say I lost.

Mrs F. Leighton
Rugby

Lucky Elephant

A friend told me that the ornamental elephant on my sideboard should point towards the door and that it was bad luck to have it pointing towards the television. I laughed at the idea, but I did turn it round as she had suggested.

Ten minutes later I won the pools.

Mrs K. Harrison
Surrey

"Why are you taking Daddy's trousers to the shops?" said my 3 year old daughter recently.

We were going to the launderette!

Mrs A. Kingsley
Dunbarton

Ladder Luck

My husband recently bought a small pair of aluminium step ladders from our local D.I.Y. centre.

Luckily I do not think there is sufficient room for anybody to walk under them.

Mrs D. McNaughton
Burnley

My father, an ex-fisherman, told me when I was a child that it was bad luck to wave to the boats as they put out to sea.

One day I did wave and his boat was immediately consumed by a large fish. Luckily we both saw the funny side.

Miss A. Howard
Whitby

"That's a big lemon," said my 3 year old daughter during a recent visit to the shops.

She was pointing to a grapefruit!

Mrs A. Kingsley
Dunbarton

I wonder why English restaurants don't serve the feet when cooking rabbits. After all, the French eat frogs' legs.

You never know, it may bring good luck to those who dared eat them.

P.A. Walton
Chesterfield

Onion Ladder

My mother, who is 69, is not a particularly superstitious person.

Consequently I do not have any stories about her which I can relate.

Mrs P. Wilson
Norwich

"Why do fish have oblong fingers with breadcrumbs on them?" said my 3 year old daughter recently. Do I get five pounds?

Mrs A. Kingsley
Dunbarton

Why not write to Britain's liveliest letters page at 'Letterbox'', Viz Comic, PO Box 1PT, Newcastle upon Tyne, NE1 1PT.

DOCTOR. I'VE EATEN SOMETHING THAT DISAGREES WITH ME

NO YOU HAVEN'T!

CD/BIZ 85

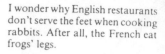

VICTOR PRATT ★ THE STUPID TWAT ★

TRY HITTING THE RECEIVER VIC. IT'S A BAD LINE

WHY? WHAT'S IT DONE?

CD CHST

© GUINNESS BOOK OF NOT VERY FUNNY TELEPHONE JOKES

Are You SEXY?

Fellas - Here's A Chance To Find Out!

What makes men sexy? What is that vital ingredient that turns women on? Is it their haircut? Or their eyes? Or perhaps the kind of trousers they wear. Even the experts are unsure.

Here's a chance for the fellas to find out just how sexy they really are. Simply answer the following questions A, B or C, tot up your final score and then see how your total compares with our experts' sex ratings.

1. Are your trousers:
   A. *Baggy round the waist*
   B. *Comfortable*
   C. *Tight and bulging*

2. Which of the following do you smoke?
   A. *No cigarettes*
   B. *Ordinary cigarettes*
   C. *Foreign cigarettes*

3. You are heading for the bus stop and a bus is about to pull away. Would you:
   A. *Run for it*
   B. *Walk and hope to catch it*
   C. *Stop and light up a cigarette*

4. If you nipped out of the house to buy a newspaper, how would you walk?
   A. *Hurriedly, tripping from time to time*
   B. *At a medium pace*
   C. *Slowly, swaying from side to side*

5. If you went out for a meal, how would you travel?
   A. *On a No.14 bus*
   B. *In a taxi*
   C. *In a flashy sports car with a throbbing engine*

6. You are in a restaurant and the waiter offers you a starter. Which of the following would you choose?
   A. *A small bowl of pea soup*
   B. *A couple of poached eggs*
   C. *An enormous wedge of juicy melon*

7. You wake up one morning feeling sexy. What would you do?
   A. *Get up and have a cold bath*
   B. *Go back to sleep*
   C. *Go out and buy a pair of leather underpants*

8. You are at the cinema watching a movie with a friend. What would you do during the interval?
   A. *Go to the lavatory*
   B. *Buy an ice lolly*
   C. *Put your sunglasses on*

9. Which of the following pets would you prefer to keep?
   A. *A parrot*
   B. *A small hampster*
   C. *Several large dogs*

10. If you went fishing, how much underwear would you put on?
    A. *Lots of warm, woolly underwear*
    B. *A small amount of underwear*
    C. *No underwear at all*

SCORING

A — 1 point

B — 2 points

C — 3 points

YOUR SEX RATINGS

Less than 10 — *Dull and unattractive.*   11 to 20 — *Rather ordinary.*
21 to 29 — *Pretty saucy.*   Maximum 30 — *Ooh la la!*

WHERE'S the TOILET?

Here's a chance for you to test your powers of observation.

Every issue we feature a photograph of a toilet taken somewhere in the UK. Do you recognise the urinals pictured below? Perhaps you've used them recently. Study the picture carefully and try to work out where it is. If you're stuck, the answer is printed below.

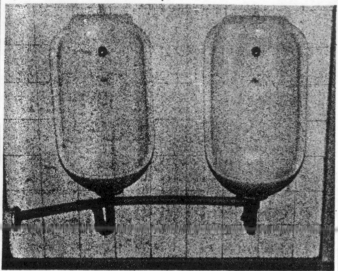

This issue's toilet is at Metro Radio, in Swalwell, Tyne and Wear.

FISH of the WEEK

What is your favourite fish? Perhaps it's haddock, herring or bass. Or maybe you're a fan of bream.

Write and tell us about the kind of fish you like. Every issue we'll be featuring a new fish as suggested by a reader. For our first 'Fish Of The Week' we have chosen carp.

No.1 Carp

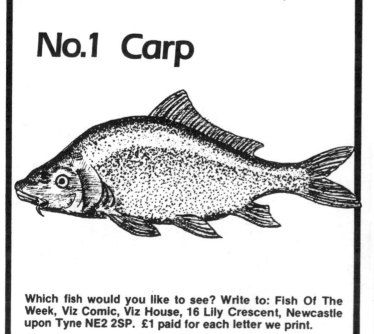

Which fish would you like to see? Write to: Fish Of The Week, Viz Comic, Viz House, 16 Lily Crescent, Newcastle upon Tyne NE2 2SP. £1 paid for each letter we print.

KILLER WASP SEX VICAR IN GAY NAZI STORM

By our INVESTIGATIVE STAFF

No Girls 'Danced Naked' In Moonlit Devil Ritual - claim

A village vicar has denied taking part in moonlit ceremonies involving naked women.

And Rev. Stanley Compton has denied allegations that he is a leading member of a gay nazi movement in the quiet village of Todhamlet.

CHILDREN

And we were unable to find any evidence to support claims that 64 year old Compton was having sex with under age children, some of them boys. But in an outhouse adjoining his home we found firewood, two buckets and a rusty lawn mower.

HORROR

Local residents told us the Rev. Compton came to the village in 1954 and has lived there ever since. They described him as a quiet man, a non-drinker who didn't socialise much but often arranged jumble sales or garden fetes.

NAKED

Reg Dixon, owner of The Golden Lion Hotel in the village told us he had never heard rumours connecting the vicar with midnight sex ceremonies. And his daughter, a shapely 16 year old, told us she was unaware of any satanic activities in the village.

Her mother, Mabel Dixon, cook at the Golden Lion, confirmed that neither she nor her daughter had ever danced naked in the flickering flames of a pagan bonfire.

AXE

A regular at the Golden Lion, village vet Norman Taylor said he was "unaware" of any local girls dancing themselves into a hypnotic frenzy in the course of a gruesome moonlit satanic ritual.

VAMPIRES

When we spoke to Rev. Compton he strongly denied any involvement with the National Front. He was however later 'unavailable' to comment on the suggestion that he was breeding giant indestructable killer wasps in a garage adjoining his home.

6

TOO YOUNG TO LOVE

I'LL SEE YOU TONIGHT DARLING. AND REMEMBER, I LOVE YOU, BRIAN

Their parents called it 'Puppy Love', but despite her tender years Camilla Johnson knew her love for Brian would last forever. And she intended to prove it...

CAMILLA. DADDY AND I THINK YOU'VE BEEN SEEING A LIITLE TOO MUCH OF BRIAN LATELY. PERHAPS IT WOULD BE BEST, IF...

OH MOTHER!

I THINK MUMMY'S RIGHT DARLING

YOU JUST DON'T UNDERSTAND. BRIAN AND I ARE IN LOVE, AND ONE DAY WE'LL BE MARRIED

IN LOVE AT YOUR AGE. YOU'RE TOO YOUNG TO KNOW THE MEANING OF THE WORD

I DO LOVE BRIAN AND ALWAYS WILL. I DON'T CARE WHAT YOU SAY

Camilla left, slamming the door behind her.

JUST LEAVE HER, SHE'LL BE ALRIGHT. SHE'S JUST SO YOUNG, THAT'S ALL

OH I DO HOPE SO

8

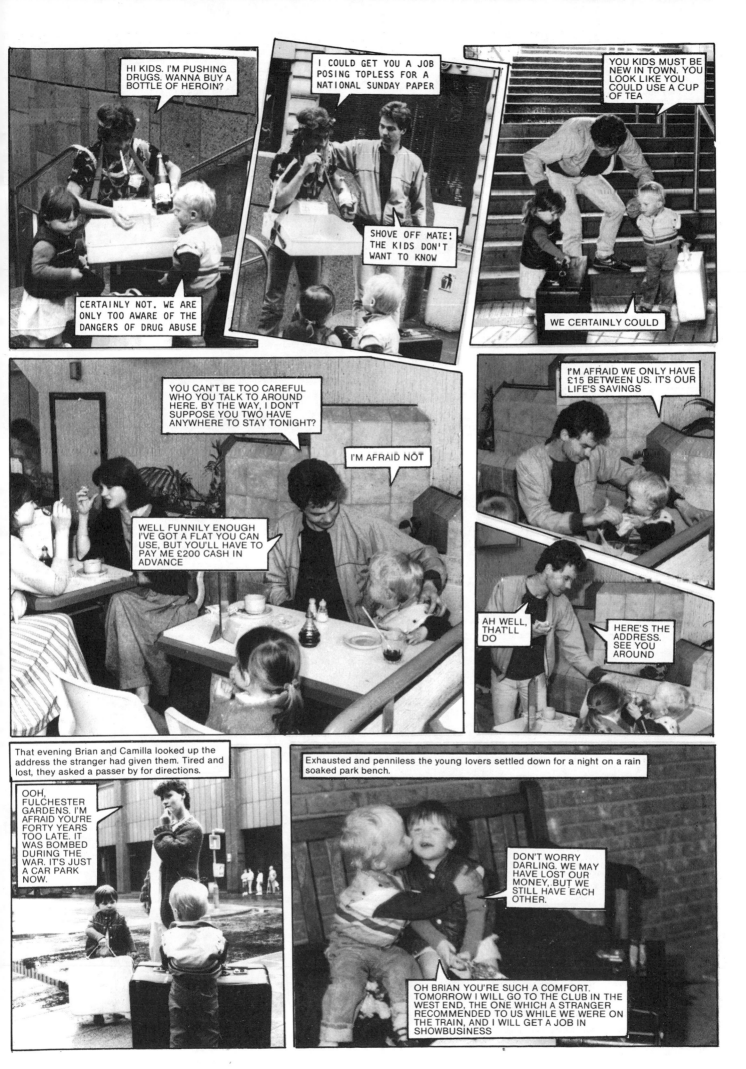

9

Photography by Colin Davison. Restaurant supplied by Quicks, Newcastle. Pub courtesy of the Trent House. Ice Cream tray appears by kind permission of Tyneside Cinema. Special thanks to Amber and Ian. CD 85.

TV TODAY

A Comprehensive Guide to all of TODAY'S TELLY

This is the telly guide you can use every day of the week! You simply fill it in yourself. Just run through the columns filling in the times and names of all tonight's programmes. Pick any star appearing on TV tonight, fix their photo in the space provided and fill in the caption below. Then you can sit back with your feet up and decide what you'll be watching on telly tonight. (Remember to write in pencil so you can re-use your telly guide tomorrow).

BBC1

Time	Programme

Closedown

BBC2

Time	Programme

Closedown

AFFIX PHOTO HERE

_____ appearing
in _____
on _____ at _____ tonight.

ITV

Time	Programme

Closedown

Channel 4

Time	Programme

Closedown

THRILL--TO THE EXCITING ADVENTURES OF "FIDO"
ONE DAY..
WHEN SUDDENLY!!!
SNIFF SNIFF
WAG WAG
THEN...
THE END
...NEXT WEEK, FIDO SNIFFS BONZO'S BOTTOM.
G.P.D '84

PLANET BORE
SIGH
MORE CRAZY ADVENTURES NEXT WEEK.

14

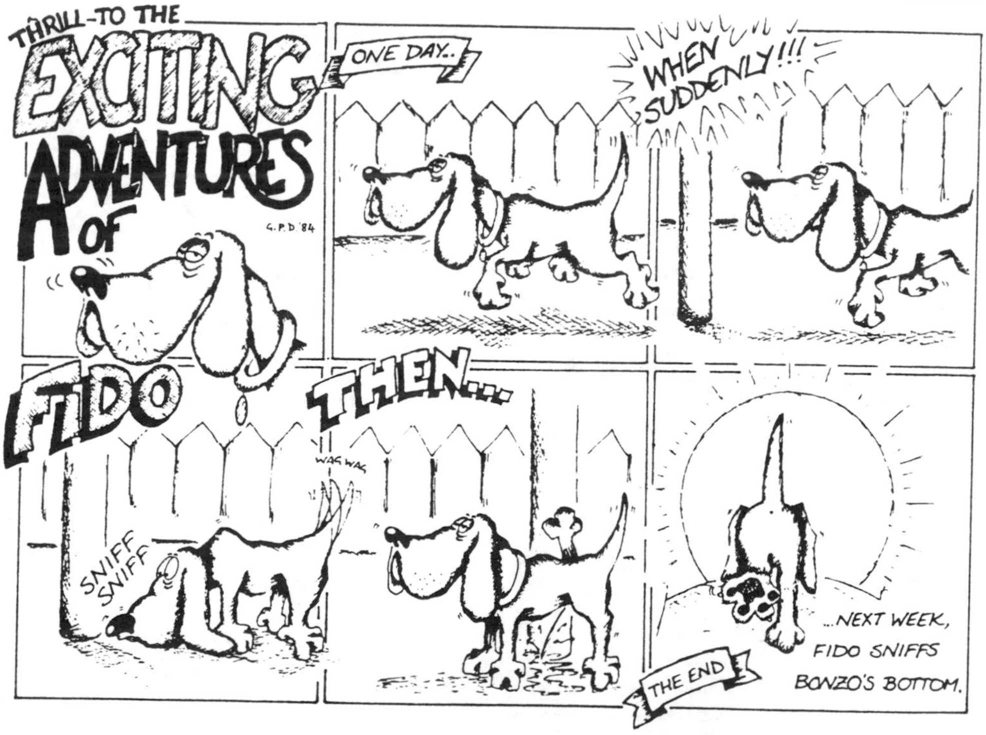

STOP THIS EVIL CRAZE
Kids in danger
by Sid Sensation

Thousands of young children could be at risk from a new and disturbing craze that is sweeping Britain, it has been claimed. For each day, more and more youngsters are turning to impersonating Jimmy Saville for their kicks. And our investigations have revealed that already the problem could be reaching alarming proportions.

We have seen evidence of youngsters dressing in silver suits, blonde wigs, wearing large amounts of jewelry and smoking cigars.

FIX

Following a tip-off our investigators called at a house in Paddington where they found several teenagers trying to 'fix it' for an eight year old girl to cross the channel on stilts. The sincerity of the situation was disturbing.

ADDICTION

Health officials are concerned that increasing numbers of children may be tempted to experiment with this dangerous addiction. There are several tell-tale signs that worried parents can look out for if they suspect their child may be involved.

VICTIM

These include the use of the term, "Now then, now then", and "How's about that then, guys and gals." To a parent, these phrases may make no sense at all, but to an early victim of the craze they are vitally important.

Victims may also begin to advertise British Rail a lot and frequently run from John O'Groats to Land's End. The addicts term this the 'publicity stunt'.

POLICE

When we contacted the Metropolitan Police a spokesman said that he was "unaware" of the problem. Meanwhile the Government's concern over the situation is shown by the fact that it hasn't really done anything about it.

FISH of the WEEK

No. 2 Lemon Sole

What is your favourite type of fish? Do you like trout or tuna, pickerel or pike? Or perhaps you're a follower of atlantic cod.

Write and tell us about your favourite fish. There's £1 paid for each letter we use. This week's prize goes to Mr. D. Woolway of Newton Abbot who suggested Lemon Sole as our second Fish Of The Week.

LetteRBoX

YOU READ THE LIVELIEST LETTERS IN VIZ

Telly Trouble

Whilst watching T.V. the other night my husband pointed out that the screen was blank.

Hardly surprising as we had forgotten to switch our television on. Luckily we both saw the funny side.

Mrs. A. Dunn
Colchester

You can keep your Burt Reynolds and your Roger Moores.

With his bright outlook and sunny spells TV weatherman Michael Fish is just my cup of tea.

Mrs P. Harper
Felixstowe

Our old washing machine is on the verge of breaking down.

Luckily we are planning to buy a new one shortly.

Mrs. I. Carter
Horesham

How I miss charming TV weatherman Jack Scott. My forecasts are always dull and overcast without him.

Mrs P. Harper
Felixstowe

I still think the Royal Family are marvellous and that they do a wonderful job.

Mrs L. Hammond
Suffolk

Cinema Trouble

Recently a friend and I decided to visit our local cinema to view a film.

Imagine our surprise to find it had been turned into a super-market 14 years ago.

J.B. Kirkham
Louth, Lincs.

★ Write and tell us your crazy cinema story. £5 for the best letter.

Mornings wouldn't be the same without my bacon, eggs and scrumptious TV weatherman Francis Wilson.

He could forecast my periods any day.

Mrs P. Harper
Felixstowe

Shopping Trouble

I dread taking my three year old son to the supermarket with me. He thinks he is helping by filling my trolley with every-thing he can lay his hands on.

However, by the time I reach the checkout I am often faced with a bill for over £300.

Mrs L. Wagstaffe
Rochester

Whenever I tune in I'm always turned on by lively TV weather-man Ian McCasgill.

His long range outlook and warm isobars are just what it takes to pressurise by overcast intervals.

Mrs P. Harper
Felixstowe

Difficulty Trouble

I wonder if any of your readers have difficulty in remembering their addresses.

I find it always helps if I write mine on a small piece of paper and keep it handy whenever I leave the house.

H. Lofthouse
Somerset

Has anything amusing, annoying or in no way interesting ever happened to you? Write and tell us. 'Letterbox', Viz Comic, PO Box 1PT, Newcastle upon Tyne, NE1 1PT.

● *In 1968 Mr K.M. Muir of Clacton, Essex grew a Straw-berry weighing in at 6 oz.*

● *Ruhubarb has the lowest calorific value of all fruit, consisting of 94.9% water.*

● *There is a 10% loss of vitamin C in all cooked fruit. Blackcurrants contain a larger amount of vitamin C than lemons.*

● *Strawberries are an expensive fruit. Their price, which depends largely upon the time of year, can be as much as £1 per punnet.*

● *In Britain each person prob-ably eats an average of around 172 oranges a year, a total value of £20.74 if they were 12p each.*

● *Citrus fruits include oranges and lemons whilst apples are a hard fruit. Rhubarb is a different kind of fruit.*

● *There is room for over 500 apples inside a mini car. In fact, there might even be room for 1,000.*

● *If the Prime Minister was to spend her entire salary on fruit, she could probably buy sufficient grapefruit to fill Wembley Stadium.*

YOU ASK WE ANSWER

Can you tell me why my fridge is cold whereas my oven is hot? Both are powered by electricity.

Mrs E. Tomlin,
Doncaster

Well Mrs Tomlin, that's really quite an easy one. All electricity is made up of positive and negative particles which are represented by plus (+) and minus (-) signs respectively. Your fridge (or refrigerator) is designed to keep things at a low temperature where as your oven is for cooking (the preparation of food by the action of heat).

For more information about electricity you can contact your local electricity board or any major branch of the post office.

Are you baffled by a phenomenan? Perhaps you can't spell a difficult word. Write to 'You Ask, We Answer', PO Box 1PT, Newcastle upon Tyne, NE1 1PT.

Sam's got big tits

A large pair of breasts

Modelling has become *big* business for sexy pin-up girl Samantha Fox.

For saucy Sam, 20, has got big tits.

BOSOMS

And photographs of Sam's bosoms are a familiar sight to readers of many of Britain's newspapers.

BLONDE

A bubbly blonde, Sam is branch-ing out into a singing career. For as well as having large breasts, Sam has recorded a record, 'Touch Me', which looks like being another *big* success.

LAZY SOD

DO IT!

I CAN'T BE BOTHERED

R.RADIO '84

18

HELLRAISER OLIVER REID TELLS HIS OWN STORY

'I CAN DRINK 75 PINTS OF BEER' I'm like an earthquake says Ollie

EXCLUSIVE

Adapted from his book
'I AM AN ATOM BOMB'
© Oliver Reid 1985

I've always had a reputation as a bit of a hellraiser. But I can't complain. I'm a pretty wild bloke. In my time I've smashed up every bar and been thrown out of every posh hotel in the world at least three times.

I was thrown out of The Savoy in London once because I kept jumping out of my twelfth floor window and landing on my head in the car park. I was trying to smash a friend's car but in the event I came back with a bulldozer and flattened the hotel.

VODKA

I happen to enjoy drinking. I drank vodka standing on my head until I was about fourteen. Nowadays I prefer 75 pints of beer, down the hatch in one. And that's nothing. I often drink twice that much without needing the toilet.

SMASH

If I go out for a meal it's as if an earthquake has hit town. I usually smash the table with my girlfriend or use the chairs as a knife and fork. In one restaurant I ordered twelve colour televisions, chewed them up and spat them in the waiter's face.

GUMPTION

My crazy diet of electrical appliances and broken glass often leads to stomach trouble. I often have to pump it myself — with a gallon of liquid Gumption and an industrial vacuum cleaner.

'I ate fourteen dolphins'

I'm pretty well known for my crazy and dangerous pranks. A friend once bet me £500 that I wouldn't eat a live goldfish. I took him along to the zoo and ate 14 dolphins before I was sick. Afterwards I ate another six.

BLEW UP

On another occasion I drank ten pints of nitroglycerine and then locked myself in a friend's washing machine. When he switched it on I blew up, destroying his entire house.

I'm also well known for going through doors without opening them. I had a 36 room mansion built for me in Hollywood without a single door in it. I prefer to make them myself by barging through the walls head first.

DAMAGE

I always pay for any damage I cause — unless I don't particularly feel like it. Being a hellraiser can turn out to be a pretty expensive business.

EXPANDS

I normally get through at least a dozen shirts a week because my body expands to twice its normal size whenever I get angry. A bit like the Incredible Hulk actually. Many friends have taken to calling me 'the Werewolf' because I can change so dramatically. Come to think of it my face does get quite hairy sometimes.

As a matter of fact there have been a few sheep found torn limb from limb in the fields near where I live. And I do get the odd bloodstain on my clothing when I wake up in the mornings.

Next week Ollie describes his X-ray vision and reveals that only kryptonite rays can kill him.

Oliver Reid is a gas fitter from Birmingham and in no way connected with Oliver Reed, the well known British film actor.

PLANET BORE....

★ Rude Kid

WOULD YOU LIKE A NEW PAIR OF SHOES DEAR?

BIG BOLLOCKS

21

STUDENTS
Free sex with the manager's wife

when you open an account with

GnatWest
The Give Us Your Money Bank

Photographs by Colin D.   *Viz Love Album No. 6. CD 9/85*

THE END

Can I have my missile back?

- asks baffled Bob

Lorry driver Bob Tucker was today appealing to heartless thieves who made off with his missile launcher late yesterday evening.

Bob, who is 27, parked his 100 ton vehicle in a Berkshire lay-by while he went to buy cigarettes from a roadside garage. But seconds later he returned to find his missile launcher gone, and with it the £20 million Cruise missile he had been carrying.

Gone

"I'd just run out of cigarettes so I stopped and popped into the shop. I was only gone for a second", he explained.

Theft

Bob, who works for the Ministry of Defence, fears that if he doesn't get the missile back, he may soon be looking for a new job.

"I can't think what anyone would want with it", he told us today after reporting the theft to local police.

Police

"It's so big and cumbersome. I doubt if it would be any use to anyone.

"Whoever it was, I just hope they have the decency to bring it back, or if not, to call the police and tell them where it is", he added.

● If anyone sees the missile launcher, which is large, green and carrying a live nuclear warhead, they should give Bob a ring on Greenham 257 or report it to their nearest police station.

"Where's my missile?" Bob with cigarettes but no missile launcher.

Wham! sizzlers

Dishy teen idol George Michael, star of pop group Wham! is a sausage freak!

Six footer George, currently on tour with partner Andrew Ridgely keeps a collection of over 5,000 sausages from all around the world at his London home.

And George never travels far without a sausage. On his present tour of the United States George has a juicy banger at hand at all times. For as well as instruments and stage gear, the band's road crew are also entrusted with six bin liners — containing George's personal sausage supply.

THE BEATLES ARE BACK!

'Fab Four' re-form -new album due

The Beatles as they were - in 1964

Yes, it's true. Fifteen years after they split up pop legends The Beatles are set to reform. And work on a new album is already underway.

Surviving members of the most successful pop group in the history of the world have consistently denied rumours that the band had been planning a comeback. But it now seems certain that the best selling artists ever in the history of popular music will soon be back in business.

LIVERPOOL

The mastermind behind the move is Johnny Johnson, a Liverpool based plumber and life long fan of the fab four. He spoke to us from a recording studio in London where work has already begun on a new Beatles L.P.

"It just seemed right after all this time that the band should get together again", he told us. "Obviously there were problems, and bearing in mind the sad

'It just seemed right after all this time'

loss of John Lennon there was a need for a new guitarist and songwriter. The obvious choice was John's son Julian, but with him living in the States there was going to be transport problems. Luckily a friend of mine plays guitar so I asked him if he would do the job".

Unfortunately none of the remaining Beatles, Paul McCartney, George Harrison and Ringo Starr were interested and so Johnson had to recruit a further three musicians before rehearsals could begin.

"I decided to do the singing myself so I really only needed another two", he explained.

LIVERPOOL

"I put an ad. in the Liverpool Echo and got fixed up with a drummer straight away. He knew a bass player who wasn't working so we signed him up and started rehearsing for the new L.P."

Although the album isn't due out until next year, recording and writing are already well under way.

"All the material on the album is going to be new stuff, and I can already see a change in musical direction beginning to come through," Johnny told us.

"The old stuff still stands the tests of time, but there's a lot of new ideas coming through and I think a few of our fans might be pleasantly surprised with the results."

STRAWBERRY

If you were too young to catch The Beatles first time round, you'll have a chance to see them on their comback tour which will be timed to coincide with the release of their new album. The L.P., which is due in the shops by mid-1986, is provisionally titled 'Strawberry Roads Tomorrow'.

professor piehead

OKAY JOE, READY TO TEST MY NEW ACID RESISTANT SOCKS!

TIME'S UP BOSS!

SIZZLE!

TICK TICK ACID

ANOTHER PARTIAL SUCCESS.

Shiloe AM '85

31

'ANTS' BOMBSHELL ROCKS THE ENTERTAINMENT WORLD

CHEGWIN'S PAINFUL SECRET

EXCLUSIVE

Keith Chegwin — not quite visible in this picture taken during last week's Saturday Superstore.

The showbusiness world has this week been shocked by the revelation that BBC TV star Keith Chegwin has no talent whatsoever.

TV viewers and celebrities alike have been stunned by Chegwin's decision to 'come out' and make public his lack of talent. And now there are fears that other stars will soon follow suit with disastrous implications for the TV industry.

INEPETITUDE

The remarkable ineptitude and lack of ability suffered by many top names in light entertainment has for years been one of the TV world's best kept secrets. For although it is widely known within the BBC and ITV that many of today's best known celebrities are totally without talent, their names have never been publicly revealed. Chegwin's decision to break this unofficial code of conduct has set alarm bells ringing through the entertainment world.

PROBLEM

"Keith felt that his problem had got to the stage where it could no longer be concealed", a source close to Chegwin reported last night. Indeed, on a recent edition of 'Saturday Superstore' viewers were shocked by Chegwin's apparent inability to tell a joke. And a former colleague told us that Chegwin's condition had been evident during the making of the

'I have no talent' says Cheggers

'Swap Shop' programme in the late seventies.

SERIOUS

"Keith always had trouble with sentences. He couldn't string them together properly. But he could always grin and laugh a lot. At that stage none of us realised what a serious problem he had. I'm very shocked and saddened to hear this news".

RUMOURS

Rumours are rife that a host of other celebrities, among them Leslie Crowther, Russel Harty and members of the Blue Peter team could now join Chegwin and confess to being talentless.

A leading TV expert last night welcomed the news of Chegwin's revelation. "The fact that A.N.T.S. — Absolutely No Talent Syndrome — has been brought into the public view can only do good in the long term. Hopefully other sufferers will now begin to come forward and seek help".

FRIEND

After visiting Chegwin at his London home yesterday a close friend told us that Keith was doing well, and was in high spirits.

CHILDREN

"He intends to continue working as before", he told us.

"He just hopes that the public will understand his difficulty and be able to accept him in future low budget children's TV programmes".

CONFUSED

When we asked a telephonist at the BBC for a comment she seemed confused, and didn't understand the question.

TOMMY ROT SAYS

EATING TURNIPS GIVES YOU PILES

MICHAEL ANGELO AND HIS INVISIBLE YO-YO

BONK!

ROGER RADIO '85

35

37

41

Photography & Creative Input by Colin D.   Viz Love Album   No. 7.   CD 10/85

FAT PEOPLE 'EAT TOO MUCH'
– Cream Buns named in Shock Food Report

Eat too much and you could get fat, according to a report published this week. Specific foods singled out for attention include cream buns, chocolate cake and jam doughnuts.

According to a survey carried out for no particular reason, many people in Britain are already overweight. And the report goes on to claim that people who are fat:

* take up more room than other people
* wear bigger clothes
* and are more likely to damage furniture.

CHOCOLATES

We took these startling claims onto the streets to gauge the public's reaction. Mrs Hilary Foster, 46, agreed that cream buns were fattening, while her friend, 40 year old Margaret Harrison claimed that she had occasionally eaten chocolates but suffered no ill effects.

Shopkeeper Paul Willis, 27, admitted that several fat people

★★★★★★

had visited his shop in the past and had purchased food items among other things. The manager of a nearby restaurant refused to comment on claims that fat people were among his best customers.

TRIFLE

A woman we later watched enter the restaurant was visibly overweight, but refused to tell us what she was eating or how heavy she was. Her husband then became abusive and we were asked to leave the premises.

SWISS ROLL

A spokesman for the British Medical Authority told us he had not seen the report, and did not wish to make any comment.

Smoking Smell

I was travelling in a friend's car when I smelt burning. I mentioned it to him and he said it was because we were passing bonfires in nearby fields.

A little later on I could still smell burning so we pulled into a lay-by.

It was only after getting out of the car that I noticed my skirt was on fire.

Mrs. P.L. Hampton
Langley, Berks.

Best of British

Last week council workmen built a new wall at the bottom of our garden.

Who said British workers were lazy?

Mrs. C. Jeffries
Wolverhampton

They say that a man's personality changes the moment he sits behind the steering wheel.

Not my husband. He died 14 years ago.

Mrs Edith Brookes
Cambridge

I was really looking forward to a five course meal which I ordered from the Chinese takeaway in our street. After an hour it still hadn't arrived.

I felt a proper fool when I realised I had walked into our neighbour's sitting room by mistake. The takeway was next door!

Mrs. E.B. Harton
Luton, Beds.

Purse Problem

On a recent visit to the supermarket I found a purse and promptly handed it in at the office. It wasn't until I arrived at the checkout that I realised it was my own.

I felt rather foolish as I returned to the office to collect it.

Mrs. D. Carr
Surrey

Funny Frogs

On a recent visit to France my wife and I were surprised to see motorists driving on the right hand side of the road as opposed to the left.

I often wonder what the French will get up to next!

P. Barker
Hyde, Cheshire

The young shop assistant looked puzzled when I asked for the latest single by Shakin' Stevens.

Hardly surprising. I was in the butchers.

Mrs. E.B. Harton
Luton, Beds.

PLANET BORE....

I WONDER WHERE HE GOT THE CHAIR FROM....

46

Several years ago my local cinema was converted into a multi-storey car park.

I still visit the cinema from time to time but have been disappointed in the lack of films being shown. The parking facilities are, however, much improved.

C. Slater
Stockport,
Greater Manchester

Potato Misunderstanding

I got a shock the day I went to the bank to ask for fifty pounds. I had walked into a nearby potato shop by mistake.

Imagine my surprise when I was handed a very large sack of potatoes.

Mrs. E.B. Harton
Luton, Beds.

Congratulations to the Queen on doing such a marvellous job, taking the time and trouble to make a speech on television so soon after finishing her Christmas dinner.

Mrs. L. Hammond
Suffolk

My husband was delighted with the electric lawn mower we queued to buy in the January sales.

He wasn't so pleased when I reminded him we don't have a lawn.

Mrs. J. Appleyard
Ipswich

A small tree standing in the corner of the room decorated with coloured lights, tinsel and baubles makes an ideal Christmas decoration.

N. Kirkpatrick
Poole, Dorset

As a smoker I find it helps to buy a new packet of cigarettes while I still have a couple left in my old packet. This way when one packet runs out I'm always sure to have another packet handy.

T. Giles
Bury

Empty cereal packets make ideal holders for toilet roll tubes and milk bottle tops which are very handy things to keep and have many uses.

Mrs. A. Ellis
Wrexham, Clwd

Send us your 'Top Tips' at Viz Comic 'Top Tips', PO Box 1PT, Newcastle upon Tyne, NE1 1PT.

Why is it that a camera lens is round but photographs come out square?

Max,
Reading, Berks.

Well spotted, Max. As you know, all light travels in straight lines from A to B, or in the case of photography from the picture to the camera. You must remember that the lens is only the front of the camera. There is also the back, and many other bits inside.

Of course photographs can be ordered in many sizes; large or small, jumbo, glossy or matt. This will depend on the size of your camera. If you require any further information you will be pleased to know that the Post Office now offer a photographic service at all their major branches.

FISH of the WEEK

No. 4   The Wobbegong

This week's choice, The Wobbegong, was made by Chris Bacon of Ealing. 'This well known squaliform of Australian waters has a frill of skin flaps bordering the mouth which serves to break up the outline of the head', writes Chris. Unfortunately we do not have a picture of the Wobbegong available.

MENSA BRAIN TEST

Here's a real brain teaser for you. Give yourself 15 minutes to solve the riddle below before turning to page 48 to check your answer

My first is in apple, but not in a pair
My second in water, and also in air
My third comes in always, but never in time
My fourth is in rhythm, but never in rhyme.

What am I?

MENSA BRAIN TEASER ANSWER (from page 47) : A smart arse

Eastenders alien naked sex romp on UFO shock

A leading clairvoyant claimed to have witnessed an amazing sex orgy involving stars of TV's "Eastenders".

SPECIAL DAY

And she claimed to have watched as stars from the hit soap opera danced naked on board an alien space ship before making love to creatures from another planet.

"They danced naked around a glowing green light as the spaceship hovered miles above the Earth's surface", she revealed.

MOST POPULAR

Later, a beautiful alien girl appeared and "Eastenders" stars were forced to take part in kinky sex acts.

BRIDE TO BE

The BBC were today making no comment on the sex allegations. However clairvoyant Mrs Ethel Gubbins later said that she may have been mistaken.

49

YOU ARE THE CUSTOMER — THE SHOPPING ABILITY TEST

YOU ENTER A FRUITEER'S SHOP TO PURCHASE THE FOLLOWING FRUIT AND VEGETABLES...

A. SMITH

½ lb CARROTS
4 APPLES
2 lb POTATOES
1 GRAPEFRUIT
¼ lb MUSHROOMS
1 MELON

MELONS ARE OUT OF SEASON, AND SO YOU SELECT 6 ORANGES INSTEAD

THAT WILL BE £2·49 PLEASE

THE BILL COMES TO A TOTAL OF £2·49

OUT OF A TOTAL OF £15 WHICH YOU HAVE IN YOUR PURSE, YOU GIVE THE ASSISTANT A £5 NOTE.

HOW MUCH CHANGE SHOULD YOU RECEIVE? (ANSWER BELOW)

ANSWER: YOUR BILL WAS FOR £2·49. THE CORRECT CHANGE FROM YOUR FIVE POUND NOTE WOULD THEREFORE BE £2·51.

WOULD YOU MAKE A POSH PRINCESS?

Are you a dish fit for Royalty?

Tasty Prince Edward - could you be cooking his bacon and eggs every morning?

Every girl dreams of marrying a prince, but it's only a small minority who end up as members of the Royal family. Today Prince Edward is the world's tastiest bachelor. But do YOU have those special qualities that would make you a dish fit for Royalty? Here's a chance for you to find out.

Complete the following test answering each question A, B or C. Then tot up your final score and find out whether YOU could one day be sitting on a throne.

1. You are at a high class party and your eyes meet with Prince Edward's across a crowded room. Would you:
   A. offer to buy him a drink
   B. wink and flash your knicker elastic
   C. smile and shyly look away

2. The Prince invites you out for a meal. Which of the following places would you suggest visiting?
   A. An Italian pizzeria
   B. A Kentucky Fried Chicken restaurant
   C. The poshest restaurant in town

3. Whilst you are engaged to marry Prince Edward a good looking milkman comments on the size of your bust. What would you do?
   A. Smile politely
   B. Invite him upstairs for a bit of slap and tickle
   C. Report him to the police

4. It's a sunny day so you go to watch horse racing at Ascot. What would you wear?
   A. A party frock
   B. A sexy bikini
   C. A fancy dress and a hat with fruit on it.

5. You are taken to the opera and during the interval Prince Edward goes to the kiosk. What would you ask for?
   A. A choc bar
   B. Pop corn
   C. Expensive sugared almonds

6. You are at a classy do and your nose starts to run. What would you do?
   A. Keep sniffing till you get home
   B. Wipe it on your sleeve
   C. Go to the toilet and wipe it on your posh handkerchief

7. At a polo match Prince Edward scores, but the referee disallows the goal. How would you react?
   A. By politely applauding
   B. By making an obscene gesture towards the referee
   C. By turning to your mate and talking pleasantly about the weather

8. You are at a Royal garden party and your hat blows off. Would you:
   A. Bend down to pick it up, cursing under your breath
   B. Dive acrobatically to to catch it, knocking a table over
   C. Quietly ask your chauffeur to go and buy you a new one

9. You are pregnant with a Royal Baby. How would you choose to have it delivered?
   A. By the ambulance driver
   B. By parcel post
   C. By the Queen's Gynaecologist

10. Which of the following names would you choose if your baby was a girl?
    A. Tracey
    B. Kelly Marie
    C. Victoria Mountbatten Waterloo Windsor Elizabeth

11. Which of the following jobs would you prefer your Royal son to have?
    A. Expensive hairdresser
    B. Spot welder
    C. A posh Admiral in the Navy

12. After a long happy reign you die. Which of these funeral services would you prefer?
    A. A small service for family only
    B. A West Indian style street celebration
    C. A sparkling military parade watched by millions live on telly

How did you do?

SCORING   A — 1 point   B — 0 points   C — 3 points

30 or over — Well done. You'll make a perfect posh princess
15 to 29 — Not bad, you have posh potential
Less than 15 — Disappointing — you're not the type

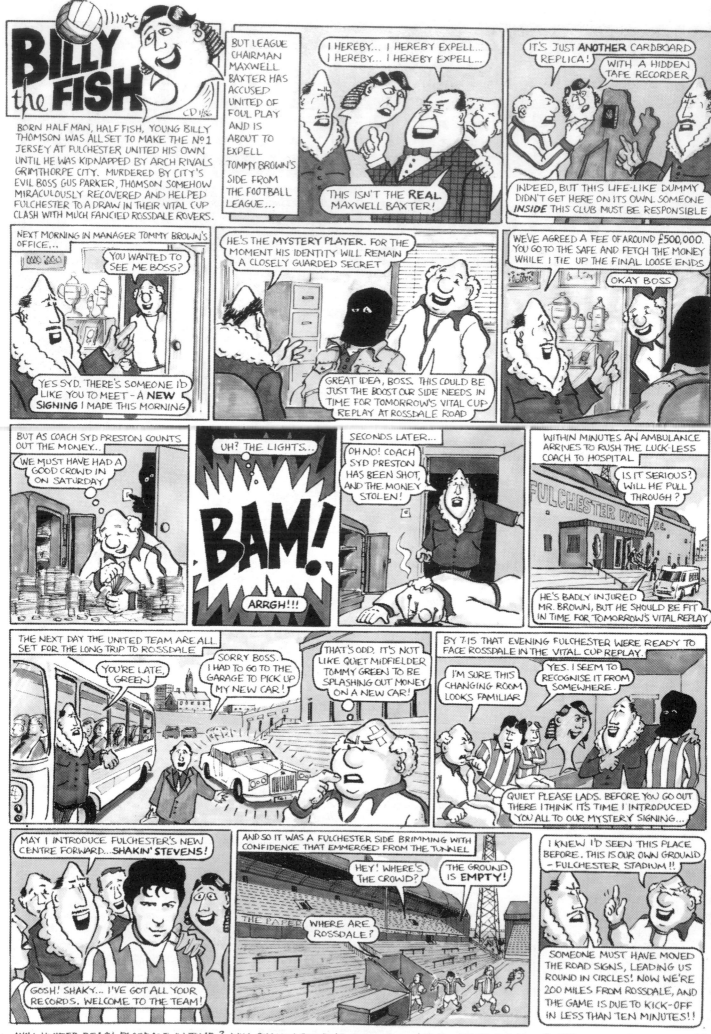

Chuck escaped only seconds before the burning ship exploded...

But he was not alone.

OH NO! MY SPACE GUN HAS JAMMED! AND THAT THING IS CLOSING IN ON ME.

WAIT A MOMENT .. HEAT! THEY CAN'T STAND HEAT. THESE MATCHES ARE MY ONLY CHANCE.

I HOPE THIS WORKS...

GRAAAAAAAAAAAAAAAAAAAAA!!!!

EEEEEEEAAAAAAAARRRRRRRGGGGGGGGGHHHHHHHH!!!!!!!

The creature's body began to twist and melt in the heat of the burning match. Soon all that remained was a puddle of steaming slime.

57

Photographs by Colin D.

HURRICANE 'IS A BOMB' BOMBSHELL

Higgins 'explosive' say experts

Higgins, with black eye, seen leaving a nightclub

Fiery snooker star Alex 'Hurricane' Higgins could blow up at any moment. That is the warning issued today by leading explosives experts.

For the 37 year old former World Champion is a walking time bomb who could literally explode without warning causing serious injury to anyone nearby.

DAMAGE

These startling claims come only weeks after Higgings, 37, was bound over to keep the peace by magistrates after an incident at his £225,000 home in which damage was caused to furniture and fittings.

EXPLOSION

At the time it was thought that Higgins had rowed with his former wife, but many pundits now believe that a small explosion had taken place.

"There are many worrying signs apparent in Higgins' behaviour", a leading army bomb disposal expert told us. "He is volatile and difficult to handle. Any sudden movement or increase in temperature and he could physically explode

with tremendous force, causing a great deal of injury or damage".

HORRIFIC

If Higgins were to explode during a snooker tournament the consequences could be horrific.

"During matches, Higgins

begins to sweat, and that means his condition is unstable. If he were to go off in a crowded arena or snooker club, there could be an appalling loss of life."

Higgins, 37, was not available for comment at his £225,000 home last night.

Fighting Aircraft of the 20th Century
No. 158 The Spitfire

Probably the best known of all fighter aircraft, over 100 of these British warplanes were built to combat the menace of the German Luftwaffers. A two winged aeroplane, the Spitfire was powered by a large engine with a propellor at the front.

letteRBoX

YOU READ THE LIVELIEST LETTERS IN VIZ

Cross with care

Last week both of our children were killed whilst crossing the road to the post office opposite our house.

Consequently we will both be much more careful when crossing this road in future.

**Mr & Mrs T. Nixon
Leeds**

Sign of the times

I thought your readers may like to see this signpost which I spotted whilst out driving recently.

I'm afraid I was unable to find any mis-spelled or amusing signs.

**T. Henderson
Cambridge**

Write to 'Letterbox' right this moment. PO Box 1PT, Newcastle upon Tyne, NE1 1PT.

Motorists mishap

After a night of heavy drinking I drove my car through a red light and into a stationary vehicle, killing the occupants.

I will certainly make a point of drinking less when out driving in future.

**P. Worthington
Sheffield**

Frisky father

You are never too old to marry. When my mother died my father moved into a rest home. Twenty-seven years later he re-married. He is now 187.

**Mrs. K. Emerson
Huddersfield**

When shopping for shoes I always write my shoe size on a small piece of card and keep it handy in my pocket. This saves me having to remove one of my shoes every time I go into a shop.

**Mrs. F. Tilbrook
Dunstable**

I wish old people would stop moaning about their pensions. It seems that nowadays even the aged are greedy.

If I was an old age pensioner I could easily manage on £5 a week. Perhaps pensions should be halved and the cash put to better use elsewhere.

**Col. T. Stockbridge-Stuart
Glenross**

Pen pal mountain

I penfriend the exciting would love to have lovely writing with. Hobbie's roller skating mountain, climbing (though not fall over!) have, also to much Wham! and Kids From Fame to the breakdanding I do. My erect is 1.35 metres, my eye 60kg brown. I have seventy three mother, sisters. On Wednesday, varnishing table legs.

**Borg Hansingborg
Norsk**

If any of our readers are looking for a penfriend, you can write to Borg at Uppsala Horvorst, Stalag 93, 56000B, 810, Norsk.

When reading a book try tearing out the pages as you read them. This saves the expense of purchasing a bookmark, and the pages can later be used for shopping lists.

**Mrs. P. Hamilton
Arbroath**

Try painting a red cross at the bottom of tea cups. When this becomes visible your cup will be empty and you may wish to have a refill.

**Mrs. I. Docherty
Carlisle**

Military memories

I spent six happy years in the army during and after the last war. But unfortunately no particularly amusing or noteworthy incidents occurred during that time.

**G. Barkworth
Kettering**

I notice that this issue of Viz costs 60p as opposed to 50p previously.

I'm sure that this was unavoidable due to increased production costs. Even at 60p Viz is still a great buy and I have placed a regular order for future issues with my newsagent.

**Mr. B. Bromley
Kent**

I have often wondered why bushes grow around the outside of fields and not in the middle.

**Chris P.
Ealing**

Well Chris, you seem to have us beaten this time. We rang the Ministry of Agriculture who told us that bushes or 'hedgerows' are always grown around the sides of fields and never in the middle. However, this is certainly not a result of recent EEC farming regulations. One farmer we spoke to told us that bushes had been growing around the edges of fields on his farm for over three generations, although he did not know why.

61

It's big hard COMPETITION TIME! Fu

D	R	O	P	A	N	C	H	O	R	G	N	U	D	B	S	S	L
E	R	I	C	H	A	R	D	T	H	E	T	H	I	R	D	H	A
D	R	O	P	P	I	N	G	S	A	N	U	S	A	O	I	A	Y
D	M	V	P	D	O	T	G	A	K	C	A	C	D	W	E	T	A
D	F	U	U	Y	F	O	N	P	P	E	E	C	O	N	T	N	L
A	I	M	T	E	O	L	P	E	O	P	O	R	N	S	A	E	O
I	P	R	E	C	O	U	E	H	M	N	A	A	K	A	R	M	G
L	O	L	T	U	E	N	R	S	S	E	R	P	S	U	Y	E	K
V	A	X	O	D	S	R	A	T	E	B	R	S	J	S	F	V	T
F	O	X	R	O	A	S	I	M	A	N	T	C	O	A	I	O	U
U	W	U	I	I	S	P	I	J	A	I	O	P	X	G	B	M	O
N	T	T	D	T	A	E	O	T	N	V	L	E	O	E	R	L	R
G	R	I	O	T	I	B	S	N	T	O	L	B	S	O	E	E	T
T	E	H	E	D	B	V	I	T	P	E	T	A	O	A	P	W	N
I	B	S	X	Y	D	W	E	E	O	V	L	R	S	A	E	O	W
O	M	T	O	R	T	E	H	T	N	O	A	I	A	L	R	B	O
N	U	H	G	U	O	R	H	T	W	O	L	L	O	F	A	D	R
S	N	E	E	R	G	R	U	O	Y	N	I	A	R	T	S	V	B

AND IN THE WINKING OF AN EYE A DRAMATIC TRANSFORMATION HAS TAKEN PLACE...

IT'S... THE BROWN BOTTLE!!

CH-CH-CH-CHEERS PAL, YA F- YA F- YAH FUKKAH!

SPOT THE MISTAKE

We asked our artist to copy the picture on the left, but he had a little too much to drink beforehand and has made several mistakes in his version on the right.

Can you spot the differences between the two pictures?

AND IN THE BLINKING OF AN EYE A VERY DRAMATIC TRANSFORMATION HAS TAKEN PLACE...

IT IS THE BROWN BOTTLE!!!

CH-CH-CH-CHEERS PAL, YA F- YA F- YAH FUCKER!

WHOSE HEAD?

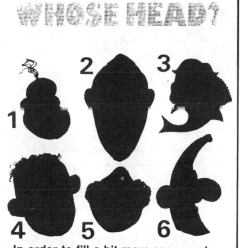

In order to fill a bit more space we've blacked out the faces of these well known characters. Do you recognise the six silhouettes? Their names are on page 125.

ROGER MELLIE'S SWEAR SQUARES

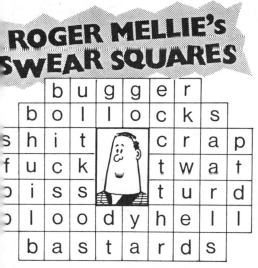

b	u	g	g	e	r		
b	o	l	l	o	c	k	s
s	h	i	t		c	r	a	p
f	u	c	k		t	w	a	t
p	i	s	s		t	u	r	d
b	l	o	o	d	y	h	e	l	l
b	a	s	t	a	r	d	s	

This isn't a game, it's just a few rude words with a picture of Roger Mellie in the middle.

DOT to DOT

One of our characters has got something to show you! Join up the dots to see what it is.

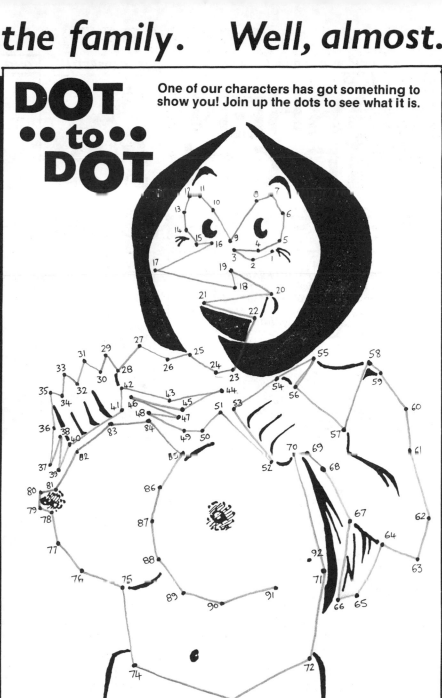

Suicidal Syd's END-IT-ALL grid

Can you fill in the ten popular methods of suicide to reveal the name of a celebrity suicide victim in the shaded squares? We've given you a few letters to get you started. If you have no luck, don't do anything drastic! Turn to page 125 for the answers.

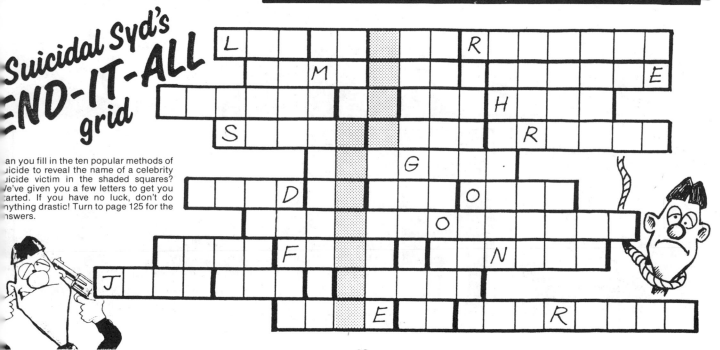

84

94

103

THE END

105

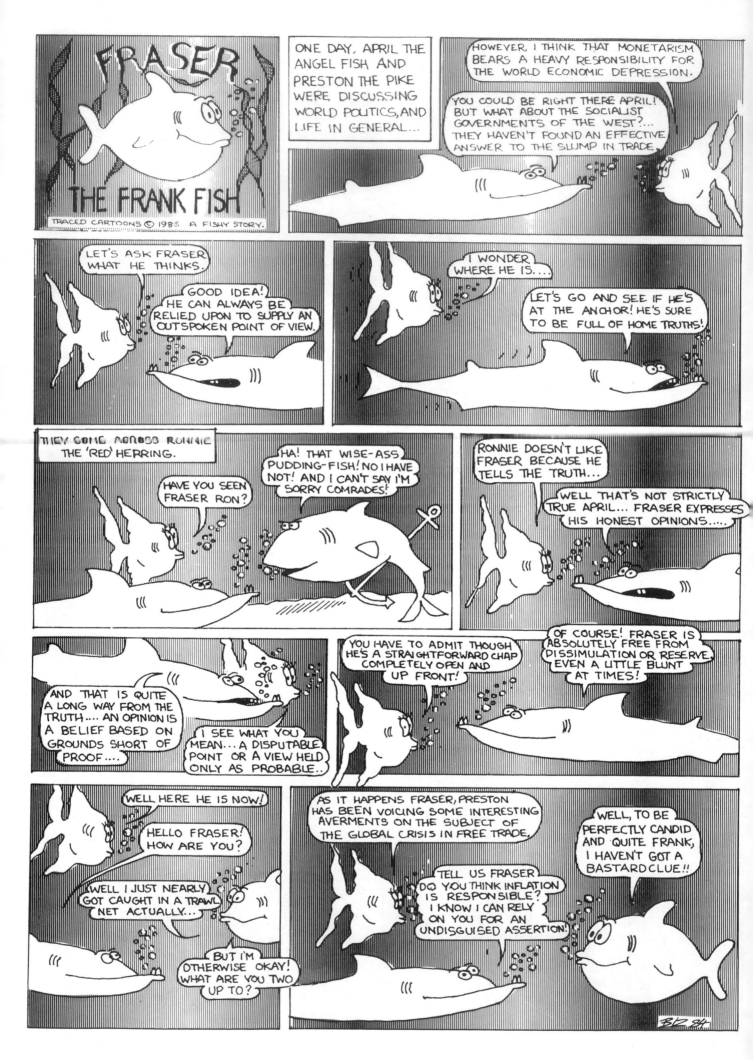

☆ PRIZE LETTER

Last Monday I awoke as ususal, prepared my lunch and put it with my school books in my satchel. I put on my uniform and merrily skipped off to the local comprehensive school. Imagine my surprise when I remembered I was a 53 year old unemployed gas fitter.

Mr .A. Brindle
Stockport

While reading the classified ads in my local newspaper I came across an advert for a toaster, a bargain at £3. Imagine my disapointment when I rang up only to find that it had already been sold.

Brent Russell
South Devon

TV Dougal Uncertainty

I always used to get confused between Robert Dougal the newsreader and Dougal the dog on the Magic Roundabout. It's just as well that neither are on TV so much these days.

S. Ternant
Cumbria

Why not include more live snooker coverage in your magazine? My favorite player is Eric Bristow. He's such a cheeky, flamboyant character.

Mrs .A. Breedy
Oldham

Having got this far in the book, you probably realise that you can write to 'Letterbox' at PO Box 1PT, Newcastle upon Tyne, etc. We sometimes award prizes for the letters which we print, although we usually don't.

I wish people would stop knocking the Post Office. When our front door fell off recently, our friendly postman suggested we get a new one.

We followed his advice and I am delighted to say that life is now back to normal once again.

C.V.
Bristol

Lucky Jog

While jogging last year a man in a car stopped and asked me for directions. I often think it was lucky for him that I decided to go out running otherwise he might well have still been lost!

M.P. Hope-Evans
Wolverhampton

Look Alike

My husband John bears a remarkable resemblance to a bus driver I once met in Leeds.

Unfortunately I do not have a photograph of the bus driver.

Mrs. T. Allison
Huddersfield

Lucky Find

On a recent trip to London I found fifty pence piece lying on the road. If the owner would like to write to me, stating exactly where and when the coin was lost, I will be happy to return it to them.

Mr.J. Randalls
Hamilton

Pound Problem

What a nuisance these £1 coins are. Yesterday I went into a shop to buy some provisions, only to be told that my £1 coin wasn't enough. This never used to happen with the old notes.

Miss .F. Carter
Dundee

Accident Luck

I recently had an accident at work and my face was burned beyond recognition by acid. It's a lucky thing my distinctive red hair survived or my wife would never have recognised me in hospital.

J. Fiddler
Kilmarnock

I thought your readers might like to hear about a rather amusing incident that occured whilst my husband and I were on holiday in France last year. If anyone is interested perhaps they could send me a stamped addressed envelope.

Mrs .W. Slater
12 Orchard View
Great Park
Rotherhyde
Essex

I am 70 years old yet have never experienced a strange or amusing coincidence. Funnily enough nor has my brother.

F. Coyle
Hammersmith

TOP TIPS

I find two lightly buttered pieces of bread put together with a piece of cheese in between makes an exciting lunchtime snack. This tasty treat is now a regular in our household. My wife Jean calls it "Jack's Cheese and Bread Snack".

Mr .J. Pewty
Leeds

Washing up liquid bottles, once empty, make ideal containers for storing petrol. By saving a few pence from my shopping allowance each week I can usually afford to by a few gallons if I see a special offer anywhere. There is always plenty of room around the house to store petrol. I keep mine under the stairs and in several large boxes on top of our wardrobe.

Mrs .S. Gray
Carlisle

When arranging kitchen furniture avoid placing tables or cupboards directly in front of a fridge or oven as these may prevent the fridge or oven doors from opening properly.

T. Barlow
Chester

When going to the toilet I find it much easier and more pleasant if I remove both my trousers and my underpants before sitting down.

F. Carruthers
Dudley

nuine human interest!

Loveable Scatterbrain Goldfish

My 6 year old son is a loveable scatterbrain. The other day I sent him out to by some coal and a goldfish. When he came back I was glad to see that he'd got what I asked for, but before I could stop him he'd put the coal in the fishtank and the goldfish on the fire. Luckily we both saw the funny side.

Mrs .C. Harcourt
Leatherhead

My husband recently lost a leg in a motorcycle accident. My 4 year old son was a little shocked to see him at first but soon regained his composure. "Cheer up daddy", he said. "Your trousers won't cost so much now."

Mrs .E. Roth
Matlock

I have a lovely grandaughter who is 7 years old. However she has not yet said anything funny or repeated any of my phrases in front of people with embarrasing results. Let's hope that she does soon.

Mrs .F. Calderhill
Silloth

REPORT SHOCK

By the year 2000 over half the world's population will have emigrated to the moon. And three in every four households will own a space rocket.

These are the astonishing predictions made in a top secret report due to be published this month.

DOLPHINS

And new technology will lead to major changes taking place in the home. Soon robot pets will be common place. Small electric dogs with flashing light bulbs on top of their heads could evenutally replace the traditional family pet.

DOGS

Shopping will be made easier too. Vast underwater supermarkets employing hundreds of highly intelligent dolphins will open on the sea bed. Computerised shopping trolleys will push themselves around the store 24 hours a day, doing your shopping, while you play snooker on Mars or stay at home and watch TV.

My Favourite Tree...

This is the first in a new series of features in which we'll be asking a few well known names to tell us which kind of tree they like most of all.

This month film producer **Sir Richard Attenborough** has chosen the Pollard Willow as his favourite tree.

In the next issue England football manager Bobby Robson reveals his choice of tree.

SAMMY SMALLS   HE RUNS INTO WALLS

READY STEADY GO!

LIKE A ROCKET, ROUND THE SUN - LOOK-OUT WALL HERE I...

COME

SMACK

the end

111

Radio-activity terror mutant death fear

Fears for public safety are increasing following reports of high level radio activity in the UK.

Dangerous levels of "Radio One" have been reported in many parts of Britain. And Department Of Environment officials have confirmed a slight increase in the number of cases of "Gary Davies" being reported recently, although they emphasized that under normal circumstances these did not constitute an immediate health risk.

HORROR

Rumours that the village of Seavington St. Mary in Somerset had been evacuated following a chronic outbreak of "Simon Bates Golden Hour" have been strenuously denied by the Home Office. However one local described how Ministry Of Agriculture officials had destroyed cattle and sheep after a radio had been left playing in a nearby field.

DEATH

A hospital spokesman in nearby Illminster later confirmed that a woman in her twenties was being treated for a mild case of "Our Tune". Although her condition was described as "comfortable", cases of "Our Tune" have in the past resulted in serious brain damage and occasionally in premature death.

Improve your GOLF AFTER THE BOMB

Well fear not; the end of civilization as we know it need not necessarily mean premature retirement to the clubhouse for the keen golfer. A post armageddon golfer can still improve his game..... even in the depths of a nuclear winter!

Here are the answers to the questions you will be asking:

"What do I do when a nuclear warning is given?"

If a major warning is given, you can bet your life that the sound of moaning from thousands of week-end golfers will rival the big bang itself! Just when you're looking forward to a brisk jaunt around the fairways you have to return to the wife and kids! But it really is safer to return indoors.

"Can I practise in my fallout shelter?"

Obviously conditions in your family refuge room will be pretty cramped, so driving and pitching will, I'm afraid, be rather impractical. But there's no reason why you can't fix up a small practise putting area to while away the time.

"When is it safe to leave the fallout shelter?"

It should be safe enough to leave your refuge room after a few days, and keen enthusiasts should have little difficulty in "getting out of the bunker"(!) Naturally your wife, if she's still alive, may object to your desire for a round of golf at this time, but remember, for your game to improve a constant routine of continuous practise is vital. (Also, remember to dump any dead relatives outside the shelter on your way out).

"Will radioactivity affect my game?"

If you find that it is taking you one or two shots more to reach the green than is usual, your game may have become 'radioactive'. Here are some tell-tale signs of a 'radioactive' game:

LOSS OF FINGERS

After a nuclear explosion you may find that some of your fingers have dropped off. This will almost certainly affect your grip.

Watch out for possible growth of a second head after nuclear attack.

Lining up a putt in your fallout shelter.

LOSS OF VISION

If you cannot see anything at all then you may have been blinded by the nuclear blast. This will almost definitely hinder your ability to judge distances accurately.

GROWTH OF A SECOND HEAD

There is nothing more annoying for the amateur golfer than someone looking over his shoulder when he attempts to play a difficult tee shot. Unfortunately, it happens all too often. However, if you fail to recognize this face as a friend or partner while on your first post nuclear outing round the fairways, then you may have grown a second head. This is a particularly annoying side effect of radiation sickness and is unlikely to help improve your performance. In this case two heads are certainly not better than one!

Loss of fingers will almost certainly affect your grip.

As well as those problems already mentioned, there may be other hazards which the post nuclear attack golfer will have to deal with. He may be already on the course when the bomb drops. How can he tell that he has heard a nuclear explosion and not, for instance, a car backfiring? Well, here are some clues:

A car backfiring may sound like a nuclear explosion, but an actual nuclear blast produces a blinding flash lasting some seconds, accompanied by searing heat and followed some seconds later by a hurricane-like blast. The effects of a car backfiring are not quite so severe.

"In the event of a nuclear attack should I return to the clubhouse or should I carry on with my game?"

If the nuclear weapon has landed directly on the golf course, there is little point in carrying on with your game. It is most likely that your clubs will have melted, and you yourself will have become a charred lump of tissue indistinguishable from a flagpole. If you do survive, you should return to the clubhouse which, incidentally, may have taken up a new position some miles from the golf course due to the aforementioned hurricane-like blast.

HE WAS KING OF THE POOL TABLE — BUT NOW HE FACED HIS TOUGHEST COMPETITION OF ALL IN .....

A CUE FOR LOVE

Since losing his job at the local factory young Mick Sidebottom had spent two unhappy years on the dole. Lonely and disillusioned with life he whiled away the hours in billiard halls and at his local pub where he had become undisputed champion of the pool table.

But the long and uneventful evenings spent playing pool had recently been brightened up by the arrival of an attractive new barmaid, Lucy Jones.

I CAN'T KEEP MY EYES OFF THAT ATTRACTIVE NEW BARMAID. SHE'S BEGINNING TO AFFECT MY CONCENTRATION.

DAMN! I'VE MIS-CUED!

WOULD YOU MIND TRYING TO KEEP THE BALLS ON THE TABLE, PAL?

SORRY MATE. I WAS DISTRACTED.

120

Photography by **C.W. Davis**

Filmed entirely on location with a came

OH WHAT A WONDERFUL WOMAN

You are fantastic Your Majesty

At 60 she is the most popular monarch in British history. The longest reigning since Queen Victoria. The most loved, respected and admired lady in the world. She is of course our noble Queen.

Despite her sixty years she remains attractive. More so than many women half her age. Many of today's young girls must enter beauty competitions wishing that they had a fraction of the Queen's charm, style and good looks. In fact, to look at her you wouldn't think she was 60. She looks more like 25.

Remarkable

Her reign has been long and victorious. Even before she came to the throne the nation was indebted to this remarkable lady. For as a wartime services volunteer the young Princess Elizabeth almost single-handedly saved London from the German blitz.

Glorious

There can be little doubt that this truly wonderful lady has the most difficult job in the world. Harder than being an astronaught or deep sea diver. Yet over her glorious 34 year reign she has performed her duties to perfection, far better than anyone else could have done. Shaking hands, visiting foreign countries, talking to lots and lots of people. Often being in two places at once, but always finding time to stop and talk to old ladies.

Cameras cannot do her justice

Despite competition from Princess Diana the Queen remains Britain's best dressed woman. Whether in a flowery hat or yellow coat, a sparkling evening gown or yellow coat, she always steals the show. Top photographers all agree that their cameras simply cannot do justice to this fantastic woman.

Charming

But as well as her charm the Queen has nerves of steel, as she showed during a recent visit to a foreign country. Suddenly, her hat blew off. A whole nation held its breath. Millions of TV viewers around the world looked on in silence. Calmly, she caught it, and put it back on her head.

Indestructable

The security hazards of public life have increased many fold in recent years, but the Queen

The Queen as we see her every day on money and (inset) wearing a hat.

never gives a thought to her personal safety. Indeed, she isn't scared of anything. We will never forget, in 1982, she was confronted by an intruder in her bedroom. A foreign King or Queen would probably have panicked. But not our Queen. "Get out of here at once!" she calmly told the man who was later arrested. He was one visitor who definitely wouldn't be going back to Buckingham Palace in a hurry!

But as well as fulfilling her public duties, changing the guards at Buckingham Palace, opening endless buildings and appearing on stamps, money and postal orders, there is a private side to the Queen. The caring mother who, in difficult times, has struggled to bring up a Royal family. With several large homes to run, and four hungry mouths to feed. Now that job is done, and her children have grown up. All of them healthy, attractive, warm and friendly people. Four majestic, glowing tributes to their outstanding glorious mother.

Brilliant

And like those children we all love the Queen. She is absolutely brilliant, and in this her sixtieth year, we raise our hats and our glasses in wishing her a further one hundred and sixty marvellous years ruling over us.

123